Ballerinas in Stained Glass
Authentic Stained Glass Patterns

Also a Unique Coloring Book

By Penny Vedrenne

Copyright 2006
All rights reserved under Pan American and International Copyright Conventions.

You may use the designs and illustrations for your own personal graphics and craft applications. Republication or reproduction of any illustration by any other graphic service, whether it be in a book or in any other design resource, is strictly prohibited.

Manufactured in the United States of America

For additional copies or for reproduction rights please contact Penny Vedrenne at pennyvedrenne@yahoo.com or P.O. Box 23061, New Orleans, La. 70183

ISBN 978-1-4303-1788-3

Publisher's Note

Ballerinas are the perfect subject to be transformed with the medium of Stained Glass because of their beauty and elegance. The gentle and graceful movements of the Dancer lend itself perfectly to the shimmering, subtle effects of glass.

This collection of 21 patterns by stained-glass artist Penny M. Vedrenne offer a variety of poses and costumes. However, all are created in similar style so that two or more panels can be combined to create a sequence.

These designs may be enlarged or reduced to suit your needs. They are readily adaptable for use in windows, doors, mirrors, lampshades and many other craft applications. This book is intended to be used in conjunction with a suitable stained-glass instruction book.

I hope you enjoy working with these patterns as much as I have enjoyed creating them for you!

A portion of the proceeds from this book will be donated to the Arts and/or Art Education.

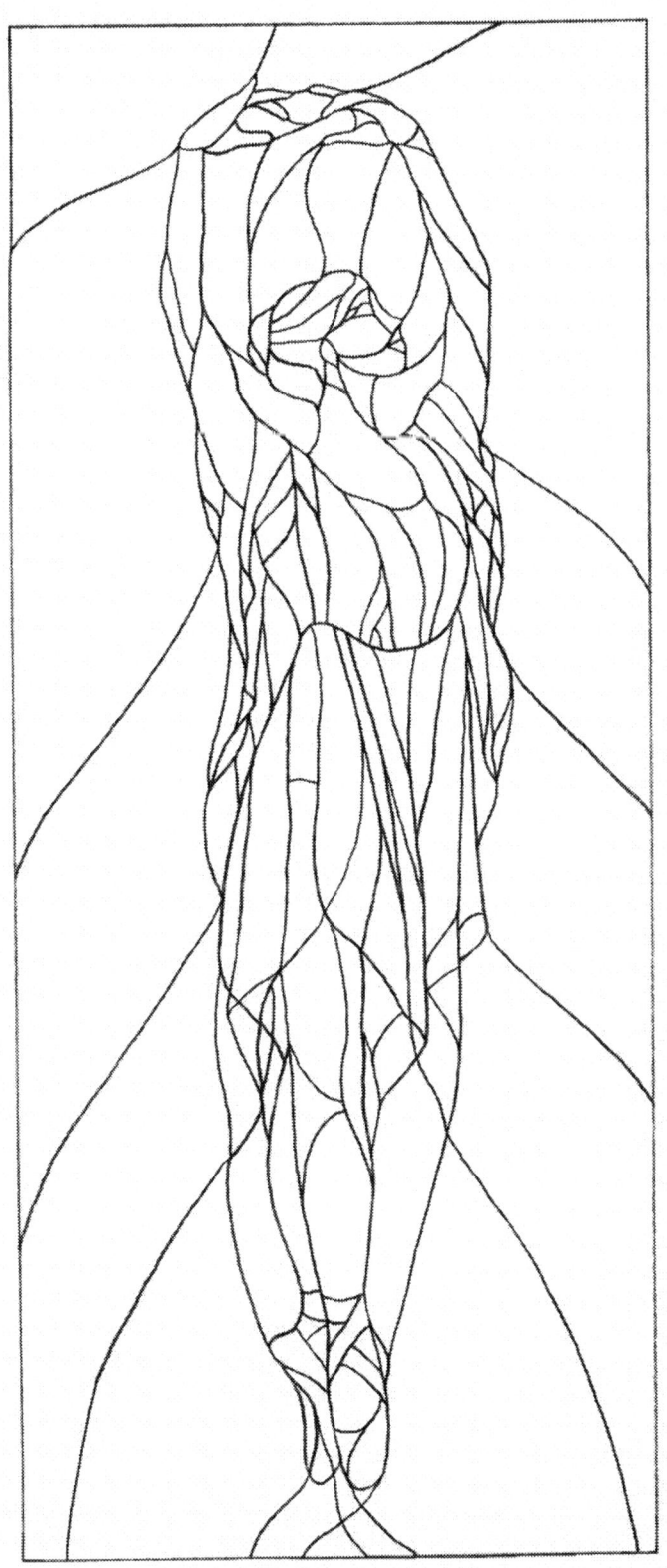

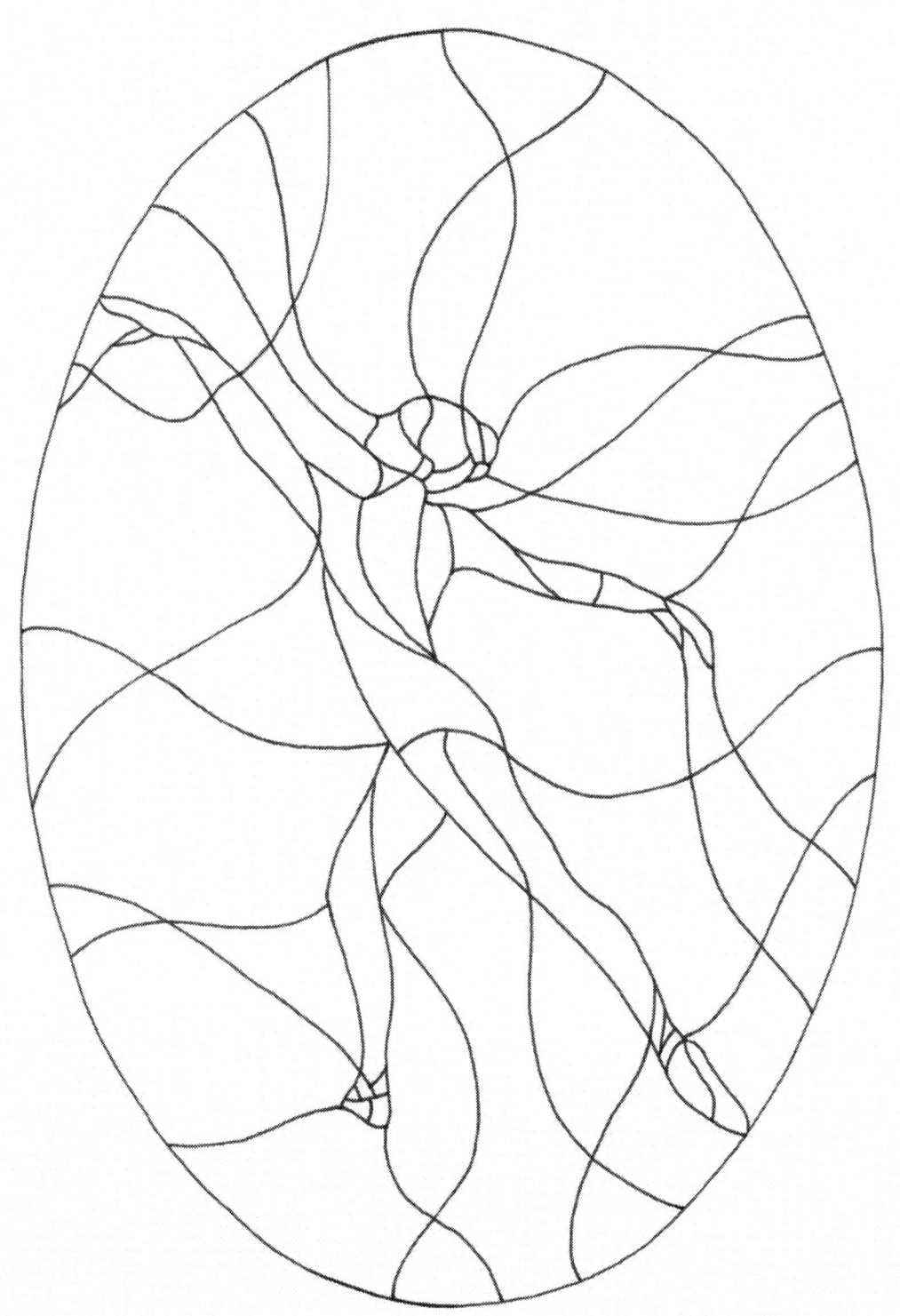

Notes:

Printed in the USA
CPSIA information can be obtained
at www.ICGtesting.com
LVHW071942110124
768803LV00015B/850